Make Money with Handmade and Vintage Goods

Thrive with Handmade and Vintage Sales Online for Artisanal Business Success

Harper Wells

Life Level Up Books, LLC

Make Money with Handmade and Vintage Goods: Thrive with Handmade and Vintage Sales Online for Artisanal Business Success

Copyright © 2024 by Harper Wells

All rights reserved.

Disclaimer Notice:

Please note the information contained within this document is for educational and entertainment purposes only. All effort has been executed to present accurate, up to date, reliable, complete information. No warranties of any kind are declared or implied. Readers acknowledge that the author is not engaged in the rendering of legal, financial, medical or professional advice. The content within this book has been derived from various sources. Please consult a licensed professional before attempting any techniques outlined in this book.

By reading this document, the reader agrees that under no circumstances is the author responsible for any losses, direct or indirect, that are incurred as a result of the use of the information contained within this document, including, but not limited to, errors, omissions, or inaccuracies.

This book is written for entertainment purposes only. The statements made in this book do not necessarily reflect the present market at the time of reading or current views of the author. Furthermore, the author accepts no responsibility for actions taken by the reader as a result of information presented in this book.

MAKE MONEY WITH HANDMADE AND VINTAGE...

No part of this book may be reproduced in any form or by any electronic or mechanical means, including information storage and retrieval systems, without written permission from the author, except for the use of brief quotations in a book review.

Contents

1. Vintage Ventures   1
2. Exploring Vintage Markets   4
3. Restoring Vintage Finds   13
4. Valuing Your Vintage Collection   21
5. Marketing Your Vintage Collection   31
6. Sourcing Vintage Internationally   39
7. Vintage Photography and Memorabilia   48
8. Vintage Fashion and Textiles   56
9. Vintage Furniture and Decor   65
10. Vintage Vehicles and Automobiles   74
11. Vintage Collectibles and Toys   82
12. Conclusion   91

Chapter 1
Vintage Ventures

Introduction

"Dive into the heart of 'Make Money with Handmade and Vintage Goods,' where yesteryear's gems are reimagined as today's successes. Here, you'll find that the charm of vintage transcends mere nostalgia, evolving into a dynamic fusion of history and contemporary enterprise. Embark on a journey with this book as your compass, navigating a route that transforms a passion for the vintage into a thriving business. This path promises not only fulfillment but also the thrill of bridging eras through your entrepreneurial spirit."

Each chapter in this book is a step on the path to mastering the art of vintage. From the thrill of the hunt in cluttered markets to the satisfaction of a successful sale, you'll learn the ins and outs of this unique business world. Whether you're a seasoned collector or a curious newcomer, these insights are tailored to fuel your passion and sharpen your skills.

The first chapter takes you through the bustling lanes of vintage markets. Here, you'll learn how to spot hidden gems and understand the emotional resonance that makes vintage items so coveted. It's not just about buying and selling; it's about connecting with a piece of history and bringing it into the present. You'll dive into the psychology behind collecting and the strategies to identify the best markets, both local and online.

Next, we roll up our sleeves and dive into the art of restoration. It's one thing to find a vintage piece, but it's another to bring it back to life. This chapter is a crash course in transforming the old into gold, balancing the authenticity of the past with the demands of the present market. You'll learn from experts on when to do it yourself and when to call in the pros, ensuring every restoration is a story worth telling.

Valuing your vintage collection is an art in itself, covered in the third chapter. Here, you'll become adept at appraisal, understanding the factors that determine an item's worth. This knowledge isn't just academic; it's crucial for making savvy business decisions. You'll also learn the importance of proper documentation and networking with other experts, making sure your collection's value is recognized and respected.

Marketing your vintage collection is an adventure through the exciting world of branding and sales. In this digital age, an engaging online presence is vital, and this chapter guides you through crafting a compelling brand story and effective digital marketing strategies. You'll learn how to capture your audience's attention, both online and offline, turning your vintage passion into a recognizable and beloved brand.

"Sourcing Vintage Internationally" opens your horizons to the global vintage scene. This chapter is your passport to understanding the nuances of international markets and navigating the logistics of global sourcing. It's a thrilling ride across cultures and continents, uncovering the secrets of the worldwide vintage community.

The later chapters dive into specialized areas such as vintage photography tips and memorabilia, fashion and textiles, furniture and decor, and even vintage vehicles and toys. Each section is packed with insights and tips on collecting, preserving, and monetizing these unique items. You'll learn not just to appreciate the beauty of these objects but also to understand their place in the broader cultural and economic landscape.

As we venture through "Vintage Ventures," remember this is more than just a guide; it's an invitation to a community. A community that values history, cherishes craftsmanship, and thrives on the thrill of the find. It's an adventure through time, where every item has a story waiting to be rediscovered and retold.

So, whether you're looking to turn a hobby into a business or simply deepen your appreciation for vintage treasures, "Vintage Ventures" is your companion on this exciting experience. Let's embark on this adventure together, uncovering the past's secrets to build a successful future.

Chapter 2
Exploring Vintage Markets

Stepping into a vintage market is like time-traveling without the need for a DeLorean. It's where history's treasures are hiding in plain sight, waiting to tell their stories to anyone willing to listen. For the uninitiated, vintage markets are not just places to buy old stuff; they're treasure troves of history, culture, and unique style. They're where the past meets the present, creating a fusion that's irresistibly cool.

Let's Debunk a Myth Right Off the Bat: vintage shopping isn't just for hipsters or your eccentric Aunt Edna. It's a playground for anyone with a taste for the unique, the story-rich, and the environmentally conscious. Yes, you're being kind to the planet by giving a second life to something that was loved before. Vintage is the original recycle, reduce, reuse - and it's far more stylish than your average blue bin.

The Art of Discovery: Unlike your predictable high street shops, every item in a vintage market has its own narrative. From a 1950s cocktail dress to a mid-century modern lamp, these pieces have lived lives before they reach you. It's not just shopping; it's an archaeological dig for fashion and decor enthusiasts.

Eco-friendly and Wallet-friendly: Buying vintage isn't just a style choice; it's an environmental statement. Vintage pieces don't contribute to the fast fashion crisis, making them a sustainable option. Plus, let's face it, finding a designer gem at a fraction of its original price is a thrill like no other.

Crafting a Unique Style: Vintage shopping allows you to develop a style that's all your own. It's a way to express your individuality without uttering a word. When you wear a vintage piece, you're not just wearing a garment; you're wearing a piece of history.

Now, let's dive into some actionable advice:

- Start Small: If you're new to vintage, start with accessories. A vintage scarf or a classic watch can add a touch of timelessness to any outfit.

- Learn the Lingo: Understand the difference between vintage, antique, and retro. It'll help you navigate the market and understand what you're looking at.

- Check the Condition: Look for signs of wear and tear. A little patina adds character, but too much damage can be a deal-breaker.

Quotes from fashion icons can be incredibly inspiring. Coco Chanel once said, "Fashion changes, but style endures." This perfectly encapsulates the essence of vintage - timeless style.

When exploring these markets, think of it as a treasure hunt. You never know what you might find. It could be a rare vinyl record, a vintage camera, or a piece of jewelry with a story to tell.

Incorporating vintage into your lifestyle isn't just about owning cool stuff. It's about embracing a piece of history and making it your own. It's a statement about who you are and what you value. And in a world of mass production and fleeting trends, choosing vintage is a bold move.

Remember that vintage shopping is more than a pastime; it's time travel into the past, a statement of sustainability, and a way to carve out your unique style. Next time you pass by a vintage market, take a moment to step in. You might just find a piece of history that resonates with your story, waiting to be a part of your experience. Remember, in the world of vintage, every piece has a story, and the next chapter is yours to write.

The Allure of Vintage: Embracing Time-Honored Treasures

Have you ever wondered what draws us to vintage items, those time-worn treasures that whisper tales of bygone eras? There's something undeniably enchanting about vintage goods, a charm that transcends the simple act of owning something old.

The Timeless Appeal of Vintage Items

a. Why Vintage Never Goes Out of Style: Vintage items, be they clothes, furniture, or collectibles, possess an enduring appeal. Each piece tells a story, a fragment of history that continues to live on. This allure stems from their uniqueness – no two vintage items are exactly alike.

b. The Craftsmanship of Yesteryears: Often, vintage items showcase the meticulous craftsmanship of the past, something that's increasingly rare in today's mass-produced world. The attention to detail and quality found in these pieces is a testament to the skills of artisans from decades ago.

Understanding the Market for Vintage Goods

a. The Growing Popularity: The vintage market has seen a resurgence, especially among younger generations. There's a growing appreciation for the sustainability and uniqueness of vintage items.

b. Navigating the Market: For newcomers, the vintage market can seem daunting. It's important to learn about the era and authenticity of items. Familiarizing yourself with the market trends and prices can also help you make informed purchases.

The Emotional Connection to Historical Pieces

a. Stories Behind the Pieces: Every vintage item has a history, a past life that adds depth and character. Owning a vintage piece is like holding a piece of history in your hands.

b. Creating a Personal Connection: Many people feel a personal connection to vintage items. They might remind you of a beloved family member or a cherished moment in history. This emotional tie adds immeasurable value to vintage goods.

Have you ever felt the thrill of finding a unique vintage item that speaks to you?

When exploring vintage items, consider their history and the stories they might tell.

Be cautious of replicas and learn how to distinguish genuine vintage pieces.

Remember, the value of a vintage item is not just in its price, but in the stories and craftsmanship it represents.

Each vintage item is more than just an object; it's a piece of history, a fragment of time that continues to live on. Embracing vintage is not just about owning something old; it's about appreciating the craftsmanship, the stories, and the emotional connections that these items bring. Whether you're a seasoned collector or new to the vintage market, the path of discovering these timeless treasures is always filled with wonder and nostalgia.

Navigating the Vintage Market Landscape: A Guide for the Modern Enthusiast

Welcome to vintage markets! Whether you're a seasoned collector or a newcomer, understanding the intricacies of this unique market is both exciting and essential. By diving into the nuances of market identification and community networking, you're stepping into a realm where history meets style, and every item tells a story.

Researching Local and Online Vintage Markets: Begin your adventure by exploring the vast array of vintage markets available. Start locally - check out flea markets, antique shops, and special events in your area. Each local market has its own flavor and specialty. Then, extend your search online. Websites like Etsy and eBay are treasure troves of vintage goods. Remember, the key here is exploration – every market has its own hidden gems!

- Key Platforms to Check: Etsy, eBay, local event listings.

- Research Tips: Look for market reviews, visit forums, and join social media groups.

Evaluating Market Potential and Demographics: Understanding the market potential and demographics is crucial. Ask yourself, who shops here? What are they looking for? Markets targeting young professionals might lean towards mid-century modern pieces, while others might specialize in Victorian era collectibles.

- Demographic Analysis: Conduct surveys or observe the crowd during your market visits.

- Market Trends: Stay updated with vintage forums and blogs to understand current trends.

Networking Within the Vintage Community: Networking is the heartbeat of the vintage world. Connect with sellers, fellow enthusiasts, and experts. Attend local events, join online forums, and participate in discussions. These connections can lead to insider knowledge, special deals, and friendships.

- Networking Avenues: Social media groups, vintage fairs, and local meetups.

- Building Relationships: Share your interests, ask questions, and offer help when possible.

While embarking on this path, you might face challenges like market saturation or difficulty in identifying authentic pieces. To counter these, develop a keen eye for quality and authenticity. Build relationships with trusted sellers and rely on the community for support and guidance.

Have you ever found yourself lost in the maze of online listings, wondering if a piece is worth the investment? Or perhaps you've felt the thrill of discovering a rare find at a local market? These experiences are what make the vintage market exhilarating.

As we weave through the vibrant tapestry of vintage markets, remember, it's not just about the items we acquire, but the stories they tell and the connections we make. This experience is as much about understanding history and culture as it is about finding that perfect piece for your collection. Here's to discovering the charm and allure of the vintage world, one market at a time.

Assessing Vintage Quality: A Guide to Authenticity, Condition, and Value

Here's a go-to guide on assessing vintage quality. Here, we'll dive into the art of distinguishing authentic vintage pieces, understanding their true value, and leveraging expert opinions. This adventure is more than just a lesson; it's an exploration of history and craftsmanship.

Inspecting for Authenticity

a. Know the Era: Start by familiarizing yourself with the era of the item. Research the design trends, materials, and manufacturing techniques of the time.

b. Check for Markings: Authentic vintage items often bear the maker's mark, patent numbers, or production dates. These can be key indicators of authenticity.

Assessing Condition

a. Examine the Wear and Tear: Look for signs of aging that align with the item's era. Uneven fading, natural wear patterns, and old repair marks can authenticate an item's age.

b. Identify Restorations: Restorations can affect value. Learn to spot modern screws in old wood, replaced parts, or fresh paint over old layers.

Understanding Value in Vintage Items

a. Rarity and Demand: Rare items or those in high demand often carry more value. Research market trends to understand what collectors are seeking.

b. Historical Significance: Items with historical significance or provenance can be more valuable. This includes items with a known history or previous famous ownership.

Leveraging Expert Opinions and Appraisals

a. Consult with Experts: Reach out to appraisers or experts in the field. They can provide insights into the item's authenticity, condition, and market value.

b. Understand Appraisal Factors: Appraisals consider age, condition, rarity, and market trends. Knowing these factors can help you understand the appraiser's evaluation.

Practical Advice on Potential Problems

- In Authenticity: Be wary of replicas. They can be convincing, so always cross-check with multiple sources or experts.

- In Condition: Over-restored items might lose value. Aim for pieces that retain their original charm.

- In Understanding Value: Market trends can fluctuate. What's valuable today might not hold the same worth tomorrow.

- In Appraisals: Choose reputable appraisers. Their credibility can significantly impact the assessment.

Have you ever wondered about the story behind a vintage item? Think about the hands it passed through and the eras it has seen. This connection to history is what makes vintage items unique.

In closing, assessing vintage quality is an intriguing mix of art and science. It involves a deep understanding of history, an eye for detail, and a respect for craftsmanship. As you embark on this chapter, remember, each vintage item holds a story, waiting to be discovered and appreciated.

Chapter 3
Restoring Vintage Finds

New is often equated with better, there's a quiet rebellion brewing in the corners of flea markets and garage sales. Here, 'old' isn't just gold; it's a canvas for creativity. Restoring vintage finds isn't merely a hobby; it's a thrilling quest to breathe new life into forgotten treasures. It's where the patina of the past meets the flair of the future.

First things first, let's bust a myth: You don't need to be a skilled artisan to start restoring vintage items. The truth is, anyone with a bit of patience, creativity, and a willingness to get their hands dirty can transform the old into something uniquely spectacular.

The Joy of Discovery: Every vintage item you restore has its own history. Think about a dusty, old chair from the 1920s. With some love and attention, it could be the statement piece in your living room, sparking conversations and admiration.

Sustainability at Its Finest: In an era of disposable culture, restoring vintage items is a small act of rebellion against the tide of mass-produced, short-lived products. It's about cherishing and respecting the craftsmanship of bygone eras.

Unleash Your Creativity: Restoring vintage finds is like having a blank canvas. You have the freedom to preserve its original charm or give it a modern twist. It's your story, your vision, and your handiwork coming together.

Here's how you can start:

1. **Start Small and Simple:** A simple wooden stool or a vintage lamp can be great first projects. You're looking for potential, not perfection.

2. **Learn as You Go:** There are ample resources online, from YouTube tutorials to online forums where enthusiasts share tips and tricks. Embrace the learning curve.

3. **The Right Tools for the Right Job:** Invest in basic restoration tools. A good quality paintbrush, sandpaper, and wood varnish can go a long way.

Remember what Steve Jobs said, "The only way to do great work is to love what you do." When you're sanding down that old bookshelf or reupholstering a vintage armchair, it's not just about the end product; it's about the process, the learning, and the satisfaction that comes from it.

Restoration is not just about fixing something; it's about reimagining it. Take, for example, a battered old trunk. With a bit of creativity, it could become a quirky coffee table or a stylish storage solution. The key is to see beyond the wear and tear to the potential that lies beneath.

But it's not all roses and rainbows. Sometimes, you'll encounter challenges. The trick is to see these not as roadblocks but as opportunities to innovate and learn. Did that paint job not turn out as expected? Consider it a chance to try out a new technique or color.

In the end, restoring vintage finds is about more than just making something look pretty again. It's about honoring the past, making a sustainable choice, and unleashing your creative potential. It's about the stories you'll tell and the memories you'll create.

Restoring vintage finds is a metaphor for life. It teaches us patience, resourcefulness, and the art of seeing beauty in imperfection. It's a process of transformation, not just for the items we restore but for ourselves as well. As you embark on this chapter, remember that each brushstroke, each nail you hammer in, and each item you breathe new life into is a testament to the enduring beauty of the past and the limitless possibilities of the future.

The Timeless Craft: Mastering the Art of Historical Restoration

Have you ever gazed at an ancient monument or a vintage artifact and marveled at its enduring beauty? This wonder is the heart of historical restoration, a practice essential for preserving the stories and splendors of our past. This guide explores the delicate balance of maintaining authenticity while integrating modern enhancements, crucial for anyone intrigued by the art of bringing history to life.

Understanding the Value of Preservation
- Assessing the Worth: Recognize the cultural, historical, and educational value of artifacts and structures.

- Public Awareness: Emphasize how preservation serves as a bridge between generations, keeping the past relevant.

Evaluating Restoration Needs
- Initial Assessment: Inspect for damages, decay, and the need for maintenance.

- Historical Integrity: Determine how restoration can maintain the original essence of the artifact or structure.

Estimating Costs and Resources
- Cost Analysis: Outline the financial aspects, including labor, materials, and unforeseen expenses.

- Resource Allocation: Identify skilled artisans and appropriate materials for authentic restoration.

Authenticity vs. Modernization
- Preserving Authenticity: Strive to retain original materials and designs, respecting the artifact's historical context.

- Incorporating Modern Techniques: Apply contemporary methods for durability and safety, without compromising historical accuracy.

Navigating Challenges in Restoration
- Overcoming Material Scarcity: Source alternative materials that closely match the originals.

- Adapting to Modern Standards: Implement safety measures and accessibility while preserving historical character.

Engaging the Community
- Public Involvement: Foster a connection between the community and their heritage.

- Educational Programs: Offer workshops and tours to educate about the importance and techniques of restoration.

Restoration is more than a technical challenge; it's a testament to our dedication to preserving the tales etched in our history. By balancing the old with the new, we not only save physical structures but also the stories they tell, ensuring that they continue to inspire and educate for generations to come.

Navigating the Path to Restoration: Unearthing Value in Revival Projects

Embarking on a path of restoration, we uncover a landscape bristling with opportunities. Identifying, prioritizing, and executing restoration projects is not just about fixing what's broken; it's about reawakening potential, where time and resources transform into lasting impact.

Scouting for Restoration Gems

A. The Art of Recognition: Begin by understanding what makes a project valuable. Is it the historical significance, the potential for community impact, or the environmental benefits? Unearth projects that resonate with these values.

B. Community Pulse: Engage with local communities. Their insights often reveal hidden gems overlooked by the conventional eye.

Calculating the Canvas

A. Resource Mapping: List out the resources - manpower, materials, and money. Be realistic about availability and access.

B. Time Tracking: Estimate timeframes not just for completion, but for each phase. Consider potential delays and have contingency plans.

Prioritizing Projects for Maximum Impact

A. Impact Analysis: Weigh the potential impact against the resources required. Does the project significantly benefit the environment, culture, or community?

B. Sequential Strategy: Sometimes, success lies in the sequence. Prioritize projects that lay the groundwork for future initiatives or those with immediate impact.

Practical Considerations

A. Overcoming Obstacles: Anticipate common hurdles like funding shortages or regulatory challenges. Develop strategies to navigate these.

B. Sustainable Practices: Ensure that your restoration approach is sustainable. Short-term fixes might lead to long-term problems.

Encouraging Community Involvement and Ownership

A. Inclusive Approach: Create avenues for community participation. Ownership breeds care and ensures the longevity of the project.

B. Educational Opportunities: Use the restoration process as a teaching tool. Engaging the young and old alike in the process instills a sense of pride and responsibility.

Assessing and Reflecting on the Completed Project

A. Impact Assessment: Once completed, evaluate the project against your initial goals. What was the impact? What lessons were learned?

B. Celebrating Success: Remember to celebrate the achievements. Acknowledging success fosters community spirit and sets the stage for future projects.

In the realm of restoration, each project is a unique story of revival and hope. As we thread through the intricacies of selecting, planning, and executing these ventures, we're not just restoring structures or landscapes; we're rekindling the spirit of places and communities. The true measure of success lies in the value these projects add to our world, leaving a legacy that resonates through time.

The Art of Restoration: Balancing DIY Enthusiasm with Professional Precision

There's a delicate dance between taking matters into your own hands and calling in the experts. For those passionate about breathing new life into old items, understanding when and how to restore them is as crucial as the restoration process itself.

Assessing the Restoration Project

a. Understanding Your Limits: Evaluate the complexity of the project. Ask yourself, can this be achieved with basic tools and skills, or does it require specialized knowledge?

b. Assessing the Item's Value: Consider both the monetary and sentimental value of the item. High-value items might be better off in the hands of professionals.

Learning Basic Restoration Skills

a. Online Resources: Leverage online tutorials and workshops to build your skill set.

b. Practice Makes Perfect: Start with small, less valuable items to hone your skills.

When to Call in the Professionals

a. Recognizing Expertise Areas: Understand which restorations are out of your league, like structural repairs or antique restorations.

b. Long-Term Investment: Consider professional restoration as an investment in preserving the item's longevity.

Finding and Vetting Professional Restorers

a. Seeking Recommendations: Ask friends or local antique shops for referrals.

b. Reviewing Credentials: Check their previous work, reviews, and credentials.

Telling the Story Behind Each Piece

a. Documenting the Process: Keep a record of the item's history and your restoration efforts.

b. Sharing the Narrative: This adds emotional value and a personal touch to the restored item.

Throughout each step, be aware of common pitfalls. DIY enthusiasts might overestimate their skills, leading to potential damage. When hiring professionals, there's a risk of choosing someone without the necessary expertise. Always approach both scenarios with thorough research and cautious optimism.

Have you ever felt the thrill of reviving an old piece of furniture, or the relief when an expert restores a treasured heirloom to its former glory? These experiences are at the heart of restoration.

To ensure accuracy and credibility, consult trusted sources such as restoration experts' blogs, DIY forums, and professional restoration service websites. These will provide a wealth of knowledge and tips.

Restoration is more than just a project; it's an adventure filled with learning, challenges, and satisfaction. Whether you choose to DIY or hire a professional, each restored piece tells a unique story. Embrace the process, learn from it, and most importantly, enjoy the transformation your efforts bring about.

Chapter 4
Valuing Your Vintage Collection

There's a certain thrill in discovering that the dusty lamp you bought for a song at a garage sale is actually a coveted designer piece from the '60s. For enthusiasts and collectors, the world of vintage is not just about owning pieces of history; it's also about understanding and valuing them. Mastering the art of appraisal is like having a superpower where you can see beyond the surface and understand the true worth of your vintage treasures.

First off, let's get one thing straight: appraising vintage items isn't something that requires a monocle and an art history degree. It's about research, passion, and a keen eye for detail. Sure, it sounds like something out of an Indiana Jones movie, but trust me, it's far more accessible.

Know Your Era: Understanding the period of your item is crucial. A Victorian-era vase is valued differently than a mid-century modern one. It's like knowing the difference between a Beatles and a Rolling Stones vinyl – both valuable, but for different reasons.

Condition is King: The better the condition, the higher the value. It's that simple. A vintage comic book still in its original plastic is going to fetch a lot more than one that's been read a hundred times.

Rarity Equals Value: The harder it is to find, the more valuable it is. Think of it like Pokémon cards; a first edition Charizard? That's the holy grail.

Let's break it down into actionable steps:

1. Research, Research, Research: Utilize every resource available – books, online databases, auction records. Information is power in the world of appraisals.

2. Network with Experts: Connect with other collectors and experts. Sometimes, the best information comes from a conversation with someone who shares your passion.

3. Condition Assessment: Learn to assess the condition of your items critically. Look for repairs, missing parts, or signs of restoration.

As Warren Buffett said, "Price is what you pay; value is what you get." In the world of vintage collecting essentials, this couldn't be more true. The price tag on an item doesn't always reflect its true value. Sometimes, the real worth lies in its historical significance, its rarity, or even its personal meaning to you.

Remember, valuing vintage items is not an exact science. It's part art, part science, and a whole lot of intuition. Sure, you might make mistakes along the way, but that's all part of the learning curve. Think of it as paying tuition in the school of vintage collecting.

And let's not forget the element of surprise. Sometimes, the most unassuming item can turn out to be the most valuable. It's like finding a diamond in the rough – literally.

But here's the thing: while it's exciting to find out your vintage find is worth a small fortune, it's important to remember why you started collecting in the first place. Was it for the love of history, the thrill of the hunt, or the joy of preserving a piece of the past? Keep that in mind, and you'll always be rich in the ways that matter.

Valuing your vintage collection is an adventure filled with discovery, learning, and sometimes, pleasant surprises. It's about more than just putting a price tag on an item; it's about understanding its story, its place in history, and its significance in the grand tapestry of time. So, the next time you hold a vintage item in your hands, remember, you're not just holding a thing; you're holding a piece of the past, a fragment of a story, and potentially, a little nugget of gold.

The Fascinating World of Appraisals: Mastering Valuation and Market Trends

Dive into the intricate and captivating realm of appraisals! Understanding the art of valuation, the impact of condition and rarity, and the dynamics of market trends is not just for experts – it's an adventure every enthusiast can embark on. This exploration offers invaluable insights, enriching your appreciation of collectibles, art, and more.

Decoding Different Valuation Methods

- Market Comparison Approach: This method involves comparing your item to similar ones in the current market. It's like finding your twin in a crowd – how similar are they, and what makes you stand out?

- Income Approach: Suited for items generating revenue, like rental properties, this approach calculates value based on potential earnings. Think of it as predicting the future success of a blockbuster movie.

- Cost Approach: Here, the focus is on what it would cost to recreate the item. A painter recreating a masterpiece – what's the expense of that endeavor?

The Role of Condition and Rarity

- Condition: The state of an item significantly impacts its value. A mint-condition comic book versus one that's been loved and read repeatedly tells a different story in value.

- Rarity: Items rare in circulation often fetch higher prices. It's like finding a four-leaf clover in a field – its uniqueness adds to its charm and value.

Keeping Up with Market Trends

- Research: Regularly read industry publications and attend auctions or exhibits. It's like keeping up with vintage fashion trends – you want to know what's hot and what's not.

- Network: Engage with collectors and experts. Their insights can be like secret ingredients in a master chef's recipe – valuable and enlightening.

Solutions on Potential Pitfalls

- Subjectivity in Valuation: Remember, appraisals can be subjective. It's essential to get multiple opinions, like seeking a second medical opinion for an important diagnosis.

- Market Volatility: The market can be unpredictable. Like a rollercoaster, it has its ups and downs. Stay informed and adaptable.

Have you ever wondered why some items skyrocket in value while others don't? Or why two seemingly similar items can have vastly different prices?

In conclusion, mastering the basics of appraisal is an enriching and engaging experience. It's about understanding not just the price but the story and significance behind each item. This knowledge not only enhances your appreciation but also equips you with the acumen to navigate the fascinating world of collectibles and art. As you dive deeper, remember, the value of an item is often more than just a number – it's a narrative of history, rarity, and the ever-changing tides of the market.

Mastering the Art of Art Collection: A Guide to Research, Documentation, and Networking

This isn't just about acquiring pieces; it's about embracing the story behind each artifact. Let's dive into how you can elevate your collection through effective research, meticulous documentation, and strategic networking.

Harnessing Online Resources and Databases

- Why It Matters: In a digital age, knowledge is power. Utilizing online resources correctly can transform your collection from good to exceptional.

- How To Do It: Start with reputable art databases and auction house records. Websites like ArtNet or the Getty Research Portal offer a treasure trove of information. But remember, not all that glitters is gold; verify your sources to ensure credibility.

Building a Comprehensive Catalog

- The Importance: Your collection is a narrative. A well-organized catalog is like a map, guiding you through its history and value.

- Steps to Success:

    a. Detail Each Piece: Note the artist, year, medium, and history.

    b. Photograph Your Collection: High-quality images can aid in appreciation and insurance matters.

    c. Digital Backup: Use software like Artwork Archive to store and manage your collection's data.

Networking with Appraisers and Experts

- Why Network: Knowledgeable insiders can offer insights that transform your understanding and appreciation of art.

- How to Network Effectively:

    a. Attend Art Fairs and Auctions: These events are not just transactional; they're social. Engage with appraisers, artists, and fellow collectors.

    b. Join Online Forums and Groups: Platforms like Collector's Corner or The Art Collector's Network are great for connecting with experts worldwide.

    c. Local Art Associations: Often overlooked, local art groups can be a goldmine for connections and knowledge.

Practical Advice and Potential Problems

- Beware of Information Overload: It's easy to get lost in a sea of data. Focus on what's relevant to your collection.

- Document Regularly: Keep your catalog up to date. It's a living document, evolving with your collection.

- Diversify Your Network: Don't just stick to one group or expert. The art world is vast and diverse; your network should be too.

Have you ever felt overwhelmed by the sheer volume of art information available? You're not alone. It's about finding the right balance between data and instinct.

As you step back, look at your collection not just as individual pieces but as a cohesive story enriched by your research, documentation, and network. Remember, each step you take in understanding your art deepens not only your appreciation but also the value of your collection. Happy collecting!

The Art of Appraisal Mastery: A Guide to Enhancing Your Skills

Welcome to property appraisal - a domain where precision, knowledge, and insight converge to determine the value of real estate. This antique market guide is tailored for those poised to dive into the nuances of appraisal, offering a roadmap to hone your skills. Whether you're a budding appraiser or seeking to deepen your expertise, this chapter promises to enrich your professional toolkit.

Enrolling in Courses and Workshops: In the ever-evolving landscape of real estate, staying ahead means constantly learning. Courses and workshops serve as your foundation, offering structured learning from seasoned professionals.

How to Proceed:

1. Research Accredited Programs: Look for courses recognized by industry bodies. This credibility is vital for your professional growth.

2. Choose Relevant Topics: From basics to specialized areas, select courses that align with your career path.

3. Interactive Learning: Opt for workshops with practical sessions. Real-world scenarios will sharpen your skills more effectively.

4. Potential Pitfall:

5. Avoid courses without practical components. Theory is essential, but appraisal is a hands-on field.

Learning from Experienced Appraisers: Learning from those who have walked the path can be invaluable. Experienced appraisers bring a wealth of knowledge and practical insights that textbooks can't offer.

How to Proceed:

1. Seek Mentorship: Identify a mentor who can guide you through the intricacies of appraisal.

2. Attend Networking Events: Engage with professionals at conferences and seminars.

3. Job Shadowing: If possible, spend a day with an experienced

appraiser to observe their workflow.

4. Potential Pitfall:

5. Ensure the experienced appraiser adheres to current standards. Techniques evolve, and outdated practices might lead you astray.

Staying Updated with Continuing Education: Appraisal is not a static field. Regulations, market trends, and methodologies change, making ongoing education crucial.

How to Proceed:

- Subscribe to Industry Publications: Stay informed about the latest trends and regulatory changes.

- Join Professional Associations: They often provide resources and updates for their members.

- Annual Refresher Courses: Make it a habit to enroll in courses that address the latest industry developments.

Do not rely solely on old credentials. The industry respects current knowledge over past achievements.

Mastering appraisal is a path of continuous learning and adaptation. By embracing structured education, learning from seasoned professionals, and staying abreast of industry changes, you position yourself at the forefront of the field. Remember, your growth as an appraiser is not just about acquiring knowledge; it's about applying it effectively in a dynamic world. The path to becoming an expert appraiser is challenging yet rewarding, and your commitment is the key to your success.

Chapter 5
Marketing Your Vintage Collection

Marketing a vintage collection isn't just about selling old stuff; it's about telling stories, evoking nostalgia, and creating a brand that resonates with people's desire for authenticity and uniqueness. In a world where everything feels mass-produced and impersonal, a well-crafted vintage brand can be like a breath of fresh air – or, let's say, like finding a rare vinyl record in a sea of digital downloads.

First and foremost, remember this: your collection isn't just a bunch of old things; it's a curated selection of stories and memories. Each piece in your collection has a tale to tell, and your job is to be the storyteller.

Know Your Audience: Just like a rock band knows their fan base, you need to know who you're marketing to. Are they nostalgic collectors, fashion-forward trendsetters, or perhaps sustainability-conscious shoppers?

Tell a Story: People love stories. Your vintage items have history; share it! That 1960s dress wasn't just made; it danced through disco halls and witnessed the Beatles' rise.

Quality Over Quantity: It's better to have a smaller collection of exceptional pieces than a warehouse full of mediocrity. Think of it as an exclusive club, not a free-for-all buffet.

Here's how to go about it:
- Create a Captivating Online Presence: Utilize social media and a sleek website to showcase your collection. Beautiful photos and engaging descriptions are a must.

- Engage with Your Community: Whether it's through social media, vintage fairs, or local events, building relationships with your audience is key.

- Be Consistent: Your brand should have a consistent look and feel across all platforms. Consistency builds trust and recognition.

Steve Jobs once said, "Marketing is about values." In the world of vintage, this couldn't be truer. Your brand isn't just selling items; it's selling a lifestyle, a set of values, and a piece of history.

Remember, in the world of vintage, rarity and condition are the kings, but presentation is the queen. A well-photographed item with a compelling description can be the difference between a sale and a missed opportunity. Think of each listing as a mini-exhibit in a museum of coolness.

And let's not forget the power of a story. That old watch? Maybe it was once owned by a world traveler. That vintage dress? Perhaps it was worn to a historic concert. These stories aren't just fluff; they're the soul of your brand.

Marketing a vintage brand also means being an educator. You're not just selling; you're also teaching people about different eras, styles, and the stories behind your items. It's about igniting a passion for the past in your audience.

Marketing your vintage collection is about more than just transactions; it's about transporting your audience to a different time, evoking emotions, and creating an experience. Your collection is unique, and your brand should be too. It's not just about what you're selling, but the stories you're telling and the memories you're creating. So go ahead, dive into the fascinating world of vintage marketing, and watch as your collection transforms from a hobby into a compelling brand story. Remember, every item has a history; it's your job to give it a voice.

The Power of Branding: Crafting Your Unique Identity

Here's an exciting tour on branding, where the art of storytelling meets the science of audience understanding to create magic. Today, we dive into the depths of how you can establish a unique brand identity, truly comprehend your audience, and craft a brand story that resonates and endures.

Establishing a Unique Brand Identity

a. Identify Your Core Values: What does your brand stand for? This isn't just about what you sell but the values you champion. Are you about innovation, tradition, sustainability? These core values are the heart of your brand identity.

b. Visual and Verbal Elements: A logo isn't just a symbol; it's a conversation starter. Your brand's visual and verbal elements - from colors to taglines - must align with your core values and speak directly to your audience.

c. Consistency is Key: Whether it's social media or your website, consistency in your brand's look and message builds trust and recognition.

Understanding Your Target Audience

a. Research is Fundamental: Dive into who your audience really is. What are their needs, desires, challenges? Use surveys, social media analytics, and market research to get a clear picture.

b. Create Personas: Personas are fictional characters that represent your ideal customers. They help you visualize and connect with your audience on a personal level.

c. Engage and Listen: Engagement isn't just about talking; it's about listening. Use social media, focus groups, and customer feedback to hear what your audience is saying.

Crafting a Compelling Brand Story

a. The Narrative of Your Brand: Your brand story isn't just history; it's the narrative that connects your values to your audience. It should be authentic, relatable, and emotionally resonant.

b. Integrate Stories Everywhere: Whether it's a product description, an about page, or social media posts, your brand story should be an integral part of all your content.

c. Evolve With Your Audience: As your audience grows and changes, so should your brand story. Keep it fresh and relevant by staying attuned to shifts in your market and audience preferences.

As we wrap up, remember that branding isn't a one-time effort but a process of continuous growth and adaptation. It's about connecting with your audience at a level where they don't just buy a product or a service; they buy into an idea, a story, and a community. Embrace the challenge, enjoy the process, and watch as your unique brand identity unfolds and thrives in the marketplace.

Digital Marketing: A Guide for the Modern Era

In today's digital world, mastering the art of digital marketing is not just an advantage, it's a necessity. This guide dive into the heart of effective digital marketing strategies, offering insights on using social media, creating an engaging website, and optimizing for SEO. It's about more than just being online; it's about being visible, engaging, and impactful.

Effective Use of Social Media

- Personalization and Engagement: Tailor your content to resonate with your audience. Share stories, interact with comments, and create a community feel.

- Consistency and Brand Voice: Establish a consistent posting schedule and maintain a brand voice that's both relatable and authentic.

Building an Engaging Website

- User Experience (UX): Focus on creating a website that's easy to navigate, visually appealing, and mobile-friendly.

- Content Quality: Ensure your website content is informative, relevant, and updated regularly to keep your audience engaged.

SEO Optimization for Increased Visibility

- Keyword Research: Understand and implement relevant keywords to improve your site's search engine rankings.

- Quality Backlinks: Build relationships with other websites to gain quality backlinks, enhancing your site's authority.

In the digital age, the effectiveness of your marketing strategies can define your success. This guide not only provides the steps to excel in digital marketing but also encourages you to think creatively and adapt to the ever-changing digital landscape. As we conclude, remember that digital marketing is ongoing and always evolving. Stay curious, stay adaptable, and watch your efforts bear fruit in this thrilling digital era.

The Hidden Power of Offline Marketing: A Step-by-Step Guide

In an era where digital marketing dominates, there's a unique charm and effectiveness in offline marketing tactics that can't be overlooked. These traditional methods can create a lasting impression. Let's dive into how you can leverage offline marketing to stand out in a digital world.

The Art of Creating Impactful Print Materials

- Understanding Your Audience: Know the preferences and interests of your target demographic. Tailor your print materials to resonate with their values and lifestyle.

- Design Essentials: Focus on eye-catching designs and clear messaging. Use colors and fonts that align with your brand identity.

- Distribution Strategy: Choose strategic locations for distribution where your target audience frequents. Quality over quantity is key.

Participating in Vintage Fairs and Events

- Selecting the Right Events: Research events that align with your brand ethos and audience interests. Vintage fairs, local festivals, and community events can be goldmines for engagement.

- Engagement Tactics: Create an interactive booth experience. Use games, giveaways, or live demonstrations to attract and engage attendees.

- Follow-up Strategy: Collect contact information and follow up with a personalized message post-event. This helps in building a lasting relationship.

Networking within Local Communities
- Identifying Networking Opportunities: Look for local business groups, community gatherings, or charity events where you can introduce your brand.

- Building Relationships: Focus on building genuine relationships rather than just selling. Understand the needs and concerns of the community.

- Community Involvement: Actively participate in community initiatives. Sponsor local events or collaborate with other local businesses for joint promotions.

Potential Challenges and Solutions
- Challenge in Print Material: Overlooking the distribution strategy can limit the reach of your print materials.

- Solution: Conduct thorough research on distribution channels that best reach your target audience.

- Challenge in Events: Standing out among many vendors can

be tough.

- Solution: Create a unique, memorable booth experience that directly engages with attendees.

- Challenge in Networking: Building trust within a community takes time.

- Solution: Be consistent in your community involvement and focus on adding value.

Ask yourself, how can your brand create a memorable experience in these offline channels? Reflect on the unique aspects of your brand that can be translated into these traditional marketing methods.

Remember that the essence of effective offline marketing lies in creating genuine connections and memorable experiences. Whether through captivating print materials, engaging event participation, or sincere community networking, the goal is to leave a lasting impression that resonates with your audience. Keep these steps in mind and watch how offline marketing can unlock new doors for your brand.

Chapter 6
Sourcing Vintage Internationally

Sourcing vintage internationally isn't just shopping; it's an adventure. It's about exploring the nooks and crannies of the world from the comfort of your home or maybe even hopping on a plane to scour foreign flea markets. This is not your average mall crawl; it's a global treasure hunt where every find has a passport full of stamps and stories.

Here's the thing about the international vintage scene: it's as diverse as the United Nations of Antiques. A 1950s French couture dress whispers a different tale than a hand-painted Japanese vase. It's about understanding and appreciating the cultural tapestry that each item brings to your collection.

Know Your Regions: Different parts of the world offer different types of vintage goods. Italy might be your go-to for luxurious vintage leather goods, while Scandinavia could be a haven for mid-century modern furniture enthusiasts.

Cultural Sensitivity: It's essential to respect the cultural origins of vintage items. Remember, you're dealing with pieces of history, not just 'old stuff.'

The Logistics: Understand customs, shipping, and handling. International sourcing isn't just about finding treasures; it's about getting them home without breaking the bank - or the item.

Now, let's get down to business:

- Research is Key: Before diving in, do your homework. Learn about the era, style, and authenticity of the items you're interested in.

- Build Relationships: Connect with local dealers and experts. They can be your eyes and ears on the ground and might give you a heads-up on that one-of-a-kind piece.

- Embrace Technology: Utilize online marketplaces and social media to find and connect with international sellers. But remember, a picture can be deceiving; always ask for details.

Steve Jobs once said, "You can't just ask customers what they want and then try to give that to them. By the time you get it built, they'll want something new." This is especially true in vintage sourcing. Sometimes, you need to trust your gut and take a leap of faith on an item that might not be on anyone's radar yet.

But let's talk about the elephant in the room: customs and shipping. They can be the bane of an international vintage hunter's existence. A great find can turn into a financial fiasco if you're not careful with shipping costs and import taxes. It's like playing Tetris with bureaucracy.

And here's a pro tip: don't underestimate the power of networking. Building relationships with international sellers can lead to better deals, rare finds, and insights into local markets. It's like having a vintage spy network at your fingertips.

Navigating the international vintage scene is like being Indiana Jones in the world of antiques. It's thrilling, challenging, and sometimes a little risky. But the rewards? They're priceless. You're not just buying vintage items; you're collecting stories, preserving history, and owning a piece of a far-off land. So pack your metaphorical suitcase, brush up on your negotiation skills, and embark on this global adventure. Remember, every vintage piece you find is a little piece of the world, bringing its history, culture, and style into your life.

Navigating the Global Vintage Tapestry: Venturing Through International Markets

This isn't just about old items; it's a cultural exploration, a business opportunity, and an adventure into diverse market dynamics. Let's embark on this fascinating venture to understand how vintage pieces tell stories that resonate across borders.

Identifying Key International Markets: First, let's pinpoint our global hotspots. Vintage isn't just about Parisian flea markets or Tokyo's fashion districts; it's a worldwide phenomenon.

a. Europe – The Classic Haven: European markets are treasure troves of vintage luxury. Think of London's Portobello Road and Paris' Les Puces.

b. Asia – Contemporary Fusion: Asian markets blend the traditional with the modern. Tokyo's Harajuku and Seoul's Dongmyo Market are hubs for vintage enthusiasts.

c. Americas – Eclectic and Diverse: From New York's Brooklyn Flea to Buenos Aires' San Telmo, these markets showcase a rich array of cultural heritage.

Understanding Cultural Significance: Each market tells a story, and understanding this is key to appreciation and success.

a. Europe's Historical Richness: European vintage is steeped in history. A 1950s Dior dress isn't just fabric; it's a piece of fashion history.

b. Asia's Blend of Eras: Asian vintage markets reflect a fusion of eras – traditional kimonos alongside retro American jeans.

c. America's Cultural Mosaic: The Americas' vintage scene mirrors its melting pot of cultures, with items ranging from Indigenous textiles to 60s Americana.

Adapting to Diverse Market Dynamics: Each market operates differently, and adapting is crucial.

a. Market Research: Understand each market's unique preferences. While Paris may love classic Chanel, Tokyo might lean towards quirky retro.

b. Building Relationships: Forge connections with local sellers and buyers. Relationships are key in these culturally rich markets.

c. Cultural Sensitivity: Be mindful of cultural significance. A vintage item might have historical value that surpasses its monetary worth.

Have you ever found a piece that spoke to you, telling a story far beyond its visual appeal? These are the finds that make the vintage experience worthwhile.

Stay true to your style but be adaptable. Trends vary across markets. What's coveted in one city might be commonplace in another. Research, adapt, and most importantly, respect the cultural heritage each item represents.

Navigating international markets can be daunting. Language barriers, differing business practices, and understanding the authenticity and value of items are common challenges.

In wrapping up, remember, vintage isn't just commerce; it's a bridge between past and present, cultures and people. As we close this chapter, consider how each item in the global vintage landscape carries a legacy, waiting to be discovered and retold. This isn't the end but a continuation of the story that vintage pieces carry, a narrative that we are now a part of.

The Art of Global Connection: Mastering International Networks

In today's interconnected era, building international networks is not just a skill, but a necessity. Whether you're an entrepreneur, a professional, or simply someone with a global mindset, understanding how to connect with global sellers, experts, and establish reliable contacts abroad can transform your career and personal growth. This guide is your roadmap to navigating the complex yet rewarding landscape of international networking.

Understanding the Global Market

- Identify Key Markets: Research and identify regions that are most relevant to your industry or interest.

- Cultural Awareness: Gain a basic understanding of cultural nuances to foster respect and effective communication.

Connecting with Global Sellers and Experts

- Online Platforms: Utilize platforms like LinkedIn, Alibaba, and global trade forums to connect with sellers and experts.

- Local Events and Conferences: Attend international trade fairs and conferences to meet industry leaders and peers.

Leveraging Online Communities
- Join Relevant Groups: Engage in online forums and social media groups related to your field.

- Active Participation: Share insights, ask questions, and offer help to establish your presence in these communities.

Establishing Reliable Contacts Abroad
- Building Trust: Understand that building trust takes time, especially across cultures.

- Follow-Up: Regular communication and follow-ups are key to maintaining these relationships.

Practical Guides on Possible Problems
- Language Barriers: Consider language courses or translation tools for better communication.

- Cultural Misunderstandings: Be open to learning and adapting to different business etiquettes.

Have you ever wondered how global leaders manage their vast networks? Or how do small businesses find trusted international partners?

Mastering the art of international networking is a path of continuous learning and adaptation. By understanding the global market, connecting with the right people, leveraging online communities, and establishing reliable contacts, you open a world of opportunities. This guide isn't just about building networks; it's about bridging cultures and fostering lasting global relationships.

Remember, the key to success in international networking lies in your approach – be curious, be respectful, and be persistent. The world is more connected than ever, and with these tools, you're ready to be a part of this global network.

The Global Trade: Navigating the Pathway of Logistics

Understanding the intricacies of this dynamic field isn't just beneficial—it's crucial for anyone looking to succeed in the international market. Let's dive in and unravel the secrets of mastering import/export regulations, shipping management, and overcoming currency and payment challenges.

Understanding Import/Export Regulations

Checklist of Regulations:

- Research country-specific regulations.

- Understand tariff codes and taxes.

- Comply with legal documentation requirements.

Every country has unique import/export rules. For example, some countries have restrictions on certain goods. It's like playing a game where each country has its own set of rules. Tariff codes are like zip codes for products; they tell customs what you're shipping. Proper documentation, such as bills of lading, is your key to smooth customs clearance.

Managing Shipping and Handling

Checklist for Shipping Management:

- Choose the right shipping method (air, sea, land).

- Pack goods securely and efficiently.

- Track shipments and ensure timely delivery.

Selecting a shipping mode is like choosing a travel route; each has its pros and cons. Think of packing as preparing for an adventure; goods need to be secure and well-organized. Tracking shipments is like keeping an eye on a moving puzzle piece, ensuring it reaches its destination.

Dealing with Currency and Payment Challenges

Checklist for Financial Management:

- Understand foreign exchange rates.

- Choose secure payment methods.

- Manage risks associated with international transactions.

Currency exchange rates can fluctuate like the ocean's tides; staying informed helps in making sound decisions. Selecting a payment method is like picking a trusted courier for your money. Mitigating risks in international payments is like having a safety net in a trapeze act.

Take note, in regulations, always double-check for updates. Regulations can change as quickly as the weather. When shipping, anticipate delays. It's better to be prepared for a storm than be caught in one unawares. Moreover, financially, hedge against currency risks. It's like having an umbrella for a rainy day.

Ever wondered why some shipments breeze through customs while others get stuck? Have you experienced the frustration of damaged goods upon arrival? How do you protect your payments against the unpredictability of foreign exchange rates?

Mastering these three key areas in global trade logistics is akin to navigating a ship through the open seas. With the right knowledge and tools, you can steer clear of common pitfalls and sail smoothly towards success. Remember, the world of global trade is constantly evolving, and staying informed and adaptable is your compass to navigating this exciting path.

Chapter 7
Vintage Photography and Memorabilia

There's something magical about vintage photography and memorabilia. It's like a time machine in a frame, transporting us to moments we never lived, to meet people we never knew. In the age of digital overload, the allure of vintage imagery lies in its tangible connection to the past - it's authentic, it's gritty, and yes, it's incredibly Instagrammable.

Let's face it, vintage photography isn't just about sepia-toned nostalgia; it's about capturing a piece of history, a frozen moment that tells a story. Whether it's a faded photo of a 1920s flapper girl or a dog-eared postcard from the Swinging Sixties, each piece holds a narrative waiting to be discovered and retold.

A Window to the Past: Vintage photos offer a glimpse into a bygone era, a peek into how people lived, loved, and looked. It's not just about the aesthetics; it's about the history and the stories behind the faces and places.

Unique Aesthetic Appeal: There's an undeniable charm in the imperfections of vintage photos – the grain, the blur, the faded colors. It's a stark contrast to today's hyper-polished, filtered digital images.

Collectible and Investment-Worthy: Collecting vintage photographs and memorabilia can also be a wise investment. As these items become rarer, their value often increases. It's like antiques roadshow, but cooler.

How to start your vintage imagery adventure:

- Research: Understand the eras, styles, and types of vintage photography. Knowledge is power, and it's also pretty handy when you're trying to distinguish a gem from a dud.

- Start Small: You don't need to break the bank. Start with small, affordable pieces and gradually work your way up.

- Condition Matters: Look for items in good condition. A little wear and tear add character, but too much can diminish value.

Ansel Adams, the father of American photography, once said, "A photograph is usually looked at - seldom looked into." This rings true for vintage imagery. It's not just about the image; it's about the story, the context, and the emotion it evokes.

Now, let's address the digital elephant in the room. In a world where filters and Photoshop reign supreme, the authenticity of vintage photography is refreshing. It's real, it's raw, and let's be honest, it's infinitely more interesting than another selfie.

Collecting vintage photos and memorabilia is also a fantastic way to connect with the past. It can be incredibly personal – maybe it's a photo of the city your grandparents grew up in, or a postcard from a place you've always wanted to visit. These items create a personal historical narrative, making history relevant and relatable.

Diving into vintage photography and memorabilia isn't just about collecting old stuff. It's about embracing history, appreciating a different kind of beauty, and understanding that every scratch and fade mark is a part of a larger story. It's about being a custodian of the past and bringing its stories into the present. So, the next time you come across a vintage photo, take a moment to look into it, not just at it. Who knows what stories you might uncover? Remember, in the world of vintage, every picture tells a story, and every story is worth telling.

The Charm of Vintage Photography: A Timeless Experience

You stumble upon a weathered photo album at a flea market, its pages brimming with stories from a bygone era. This is the allure of vintage photography, a portal to the past, offering a tangible connection to histories and cultures that shaped our world. This chapter dives into the enigmatic charm of vintage photography, guiding you through its rich history, diverse styles, and the art of preservation.

Understanding the Appeal

Historical Significance: Vintage photographs are not just images; they are historical artifacts. Each photo captures a moment in time, offering a glimpse into the lives, fashion, and environments of the past.

Artistic Styles: From the sepia tones of the Victorian era to the vivid hues of mid-20th-century Kodachrome, each period in photography has its unique aesthetic. Understanding these styles is crucial to appreciating the art form.

Emotional Connection: There's an undeniable nostalgia that comes with vintage photos. They evoke a sense of wonder and curiosity about the stories behind the faces and places captured.

Differentiating Eras and Styles

Early Photography (1839-1900): Explore the dawn of photography - Daguerreotypes, Ambrotypes, and Tintypes, characterized by their distinctive clarity and depth.

The Golden Age (1900-1950): This era saw the rise of film photography and iconic styles like the glamorous Hollywood portraits and candid street photography.

The Color Revolution (1950s-1970s): Dive into the era when color photography became mainstream, bringing a new vibrancy and realism to images.

Preserving Vintage Photographs

Handling and Storage: Learn the dos and don'ts of handling vintage photos. Store them in acid-free albums away from light and humidity to prevent deterioration.

Restoration Techniques: Discover how minor restorations can breathe new life into faded or damaged photographs, all while maintaining their original character.

Digitization: Digitizing old photos not only preserves them but also makes it easier to share these treasures with others.

Practical Insights

- Identifying Unknown Photos: Tips on using clues like fashion, photo type, and studio stamps to date unidentified photographs.

- Potential Problems: Watch out for common issues like silver mirroring, foxing, or water damage, and how to address them.

Have you ever found an old photograph and wondered about the story behind it?

How can the style of a vintage photograph tell you about the era it was taken?

Embarking through vintage photography is not just about admiring old pictures; it's about connecting with history, art, and personal stories. Whether you're a collector, a history enthusiast, or simply someone who appreciates the beauty of yesteryears, understanding and preserving these visual narratives is a rewarding experience. Remember, each photograph is a fragment of history, a piece of art, and a slice of life, all captured in a single moment.

Collecting Vintage Memorabilia: A Guide to Treasure Hunting

This isn't just about hoarding old items; it's about embracing history, understanding value, and curating a collection that tells a story. Whether you're a budding collector or looking to refine your expertise, this guide is your companion in navigating the thrilling experience of memorabilia collection.

Identifying Valuable Memorabilia Items

- Look for Rarity: The fewer items available, the more valuable they potentially are.

- Historical Significance: Items linked to significant events or personalities often hold more value.

- Condition Matters: A well-preserved item is usually more valuable than one in poor condition.

Always research the item's background. Was it part of a limited edition? Does it have a story? Be aware of fakes – a common issue in memorabilia collection.

Building a Thematic Collection

- Choose a Theme: Start with what fascinates you. It could be sports, music, cinema, or anything that sparks your interest.

- Stay Focused: Resist the temptation to collect everything. A focused collection is more impressive and easier to manage.

Over-diversifying your collection can dilute its value. Stay true to your theme to build a cohesive collection.

Authenticating and Appraising Memorabilia

- Seek Expert Opinion: Don't shy away from consulting with appraisers or seasoned collectors.

- Documentation is Key: Certificates of authenticity, provenance records, and original packaging can significantly enhance an item's credibility and value.

Join online forums or local collector groups. They are goldmines for information and can guide you in authenticating items.

Have you ever wondered what stories your memorabilia could tell? Or pondered the thrill of hunting down that rare, coveted item? Remember, collecting is not just about possession; it's about passion, patience, and persistence. As you embark on this chapter, let your curiosity lead the way and your keen eye for detail guide your choices. With these insights, you're well-equipped to build a collection that's not only valuable but also a reflection of your unique interests and stories.

Remember, every piece in your collection is a fragment of history, a snippet of someone's story, and now, a part of your legacy. Happy collecting!

Digital Time Capsules: Preserving Memories through Digital Archiving

Think about a place where your cherished moments, the faded photographs tucked away in family albums, could be brought back to life and shared with generations to come. This is the realm of digital archiving and presentation, a modern-day treasure trove of memories.

Digitizing Vintage Photos for Preservation

Checklist:

- Scanner or high-quality camera
- Photo editing software
- Digital storage (cloud or external hard drive)

Use a scanner or camera to capture high-resolution images of your vintage photos. Edit these digital images to enhance clarity and color, ensuring they resemble the original as closely as possible. Store these digital files in multiple places, such as an external hard drive or cloud storage, for safekeeping.

Creating Digital Galleries and Displays

Checklist:

- Digital photo frame or gallery software
- Thematic organization (by date, event, etc.)

Use digital frames or gallery software to create thematic displays of your digitized photos. Organize the photos in meaningful ways, like chronological order or by significant life events, to tell a story.

Sharing Your Collection Online

Checklist:

- Online platform (social media, personal website, etc.)

- Privacy settings understanding

Choose an online platform that aligns with your sharing preferences. Be mindful of privacy settings to control who sees your digital photo collection.

Practical Advices

- Potential Problems: Fading of original photos, technical issues with digital storage.

- Solutions: Regularly update and back up digital files, handle original photos carefully to prevent further damage.

Have you ever stumbled upon a photo that instantly transported you back in time? That's the power of preserving memories.

As we weave through the digital age, the art of preserving memories through digital archiving becomes more than a task; it becomes a path of reconnecting with our past. By digitizing, displaying, and sharing our vintage photos, we not only safeguard these precious memories but also share our rich, personal histories with the world. In this digital era, every photo tells a story, and it's our privilege to keep these stories alive for generations to witness.

Chapter 8
Vintage Fashion and Textiles

Wearing vintage fashion isn't just a style choice; it's a time-traveling expedition to the past, bringing a unique flair to the present. It's about finding those one-of-a-kind pieces that no one else has and telling a story with every outfit. For the modern trendsetter, vintage is not just old clothes; it's a goldmine of style, sustainability, and self-expression.

Now, let's get one thing straight: vintage fashion isn't about dressing like you're an extra in a period drama (unless that's your vibe, of course). It's about incorporating timeless pieces into modern wardrobes in a way that's chic, unique, and personal.

Timeless Style: Vintage fashion transcends time. A 1950s Dior dress or a 1970s leather jacket isn't just clothing; it's a piece of fashion history.

Sustainability Factor: In an age of fast fashion, vintage is the ultimate eco-friendly choice. It's about reusing and repurposing, reducing the demand for new, mass-produced items.

The Hunt: Finding vintage treasures is half the fun. It's like a fashion scavenger hunt where the prize is a piece of wearable art.

Here's how to nail the vintage fashion game:

- Mix and Match: Pair vintage pieces with modern staples. A vintage silk blouse with high-waisted jeans? Chef's kiss!

- Know Your Eras: Understand different fashion eras. This helps in choosing pieces that reflect your personal style.

- Condition and Care: Always check the condition. Remember, these clothes have a past, so treat them with love and care.

"Fashion fades, style is eternal," Yves Saint Laurent once said. Vintage fashion epitomizes this. It's not about trends; it's about timeless style.

Let's talk about the elephant in the room: the 'musty' stigma. Yes, some vintage clothes come with a unique scent, but that's nothing a good dry clean can't fix. Think of it as a rite of passage into the world of vintage.

Vintage fashion also offers the thrill of the hunt. There's a special kind of joy in scouring thrift stores, estate sales, and online marketplaces for that perfect, one-of-a-kind piece. It's the fashion equivalent of finding a needle in a haystack.

But it's not just about the clothes; it's about the stories they tell. Each piece in your vintage collection has a history, a previous life. Who knows? That 1960s cocktail dress might have danced at Studio 54 or witnessed the Beatles' first American tour.

Incorporating vintage fashion into your wardrobe isn't just a style choice; it's a statement. It says you value quality over quantity, history over immediacy, and individuality over conformity. It's about creating a personal style that's as unique as you are.

Vintage fashion and textiles offer a rich tapestry of history, style, and sustainability. By embracing vintage, you're not just making a fashion statement; you're telling a story, making an eco-friendly choice, and standing out from the crowd. So next time you're contemplating a vintage piece, remember it's more than just clothing; it's a piece of history, a work of art, and a step towards a more sustainable future. Vintage isn't just fashion; it's a lifestyle. Embrace it, and let your style tell your story.

Unraveling the Threads: The Evolution of Vintage Fashion

Let's venture through the tapestry of time, where each thread weaves the fascinating tale of vintage fashion. This exploration is not just about the clothes; it's a deep dive into the cultural impact and the timeless pieces that have shaped our style today. Let's unravel the mysteries of vintage fashion and discover how it continues to influence the modern wardrobe.

Iconic Fashion Trends Through the Ages

- The Roaring Twenties: A revolution in women's fashion with flapper dresses.

- The Fabulous Fifties: The era of cinched waists and full skirts.

- The Swinging Sixties: Mini skirts and mod styles take the stage.

- The Eclectic Eighties: A mix of punk, power suits, and neon excess.

The Cultural Impact of Vintage Styles
- Post-War Fashion: Reflecting societal changes post-WWII.
- The Youth Revolution: How the 60s and 70s styles mirrored youth culture.
- Fashion as Rebellion: The punk movement of the late 70s and 80s.

Identifying Timeless Fashion Pieces
- The Little Black Dress: A staple since the 1920s.
- Denim Jeans: From workwear to fashion must-have.
- Leather Jacket: The symbol of cool through the decades.

Each era's style is backed by historical contexts and fashion evolution studies, ensuring an authentic and insightful exploration.

Understanding vintage fashion isn't just about knowing the trends; it's about recognizing quality, authenticity, and the pitfalls of fast fashion imitations.

Have you ever wondered why certain styles make a comeback? Or how a simple jacket can represent an entire cultural movement?

Throughout this guide, we'll reference fashion historians, archival fashion magazines, and cultural studies to enrich our understanding.

As we stitch together the past and present of fashion, we recognize that vintage isn't just a style; it's a story. It's a narrative of resilience, creativity, and cultural shifts. In embracing vintage fashion, we don't just wear clothes; we wear history.

This exploration, while detailed, is just the tip of the fashion iceberg. There's a world of fabric, patterns, and styles waiting to be discovered and reimagined. As we conclude, remember that fashion is not just about what you wear; it's about expressing who you are and where we've come from. Vintage fashion is timeless, not just in style but in its ability to tell the stories of our past and inspire our future.

Mastering the Art of Vintage Fashion Curation: Unveiling the Secrets of Timeless Style and Historical Elegance

Sourcing and curating vintage fashion is like being a treasure hunter, where every piece has a story, and the collection is a tapestry of historical elegance. This guide is designed to unravel the secrets of finding unique fashion items globally and weaving them into a cohesive vintage collection. It's not just about clothes; it's about preserving and celebrating history.

The Hunt for Unique Fashion Gems

- Global Exploration: Start by researching local vintage stores, thrift shops, and estate sales in different regions. Each place has its own history and style, offering a unique selection of vintage pieces.

- Online Platforms: Utilize online marketplaces and social media platforms. Instagram and Etsy are treasure troves for unique vintage finds.

- Travel and Culture: If possible, travel to different countries. Vintage fashion is deeply rooted in cultural history, and experiencing it firsthand can be invaluable.

Curating a Cohesive Collection

- Defining Your Style: Identify a theme or era that resonates with you. It could be the roaring '20s or the eclectic '80s.

- Quality over Quantity: Focus on the condition and authenticity of the items. It's better to have a few standout pieces than a cluttered collection of mediocre items.

- Storytelling Through Fashion: Each piece in your collection should tell a story. Aim for diversity yet harmony in your collection.

Building Relationships with Suppliers

- Networking: Attend fashion shows, vintage fairs, and auctions. Networking is key to establishing relationships with suppliers and fellow collectors.

- Mutual Respect and Trust: Always be respectful and fair in your dealings. Building trust is essential for long-term relationships.

- Knowledge Sharing: Engage in conversations about fashion history and trends. Suppliers appreciate knowledgeable and passionate clients.

Solutions on Potential Problems

- Budgeting: Vintage fashion can be expensive. Set a budget and stick to it to avoid financial strain.

- Authenticity Checks: Beware of fakes. Learn how to identify authentic vintage pieces.

- Care and Maintenance: Vintage items require special care. Learn about proper storage and maintenance to preserve their quality.

Have you ever stumbled upon a vintage piece and felt like you discovered a piece of history? That feeling is what makes vintage fashion curation so thrilling.

As you dive into vintage fashion, remember that each piece you choose is a fragment of history, a story waiting to be told. Your collection is not just an assortment of garments; it's a curated museum of fashion history that you have the privilege to preserve and showcase. Happy hunting!

The Art of Time: Preserving Vintage Textiles

Understanding how to care for these treasures not only connects us with history but also enriches our appreciation for craftsmanship. Let's dive into the techniques and secrets of maintaining and restoring these delicate pieces of history.

Understanding Vintage Textiles: Vintage textiles are more than just fabric; they are stories woven into threads. From your grandmother's wedding dress to an antique tapestry, each piece holds a unique tale.

The Basics of Preservation

a. Environment Control: Keep your textiles in a stable, dry environment. Fluctuations in temperature and humidity can be detrimental.

b. Avoiding Sunlight: Direct sunlight can fade colors and weaken fibers. Store textiles away from direct light sources.

Storing Textiles to Preserve Quality

a. Clean Before Storing: Ensure the textile is clean. Dirt and oils can cause long-term damage.

b. Proper Storage Materials: Use acid-free boxes and tissue paper to prevent deterioration. Avoid plastic containers which can trap moisture.

Handling with Care

a. Gentle Touch: Always handle textiles with clean, dry hands or white cotton gloves.

b. Supporting the Fabric: When moving larger textiles, support them fully to avoid stress on the fibers.

Displaying with Pride

a. Secure Mounting: When displaying, use archival-quality materials for mounting or framing.

b. Rotation: Rotate displayed textiles periodically to reduce wear and exposure to environmental factors.

Restoration Techniques

a. Knowing When to Seek Professional Help: Some classic car restoration is best left to professionals, especially when dealing with fragile or highly valuable items.

b. Minor Repairs: For small tears or loose threads, use techniques that are reversible and don't alter the original fabric.

Navigating Challenges

a. Moths and Pests: Regularly inspect for signs of pests. Use non-chemical means like freezing to deal with infestations.

b. Water Damage: In case of water exposure, dry the textile flat and seek professional advice if necessary.

Engaging with History: Connect with the story of each textile. Whether it's a dress from the 1920s or a military uniform, each piece tells a part of our collective history. This connection not only enriches your understanding but also motivates proper care.

Learning and Sharing

a. Research: Dive into the history of textiles to better understand their context and value.

b. Community Engagement: Share your experiences and learn from others in vintage textile communities, both online and offline.

In preserving vintage textiles, we are not just taking care of fabric; we are safeguarding stories and keeping history alive. Through careful storage, handling, and restoration, these textiles can continue to be a source of beauty and inspiration for generations to come. Remember, each thread holds a story, and it's our privilege to preserve it.

Chapter 9
Vintage Furniture and Decor

Incorporating vintage furniture and decor into modern spaces isn't just about making a style statement; it's about weaving a tapestry of history and personality into your everyday surroundings. Think about a sleek, contemporary room accented by a rich, mahogany 1920s bureau, telling tales of times when letters were handwritten and desks were a symbol of stories yet to be told. This isn't just decorating; it's storytelling through design.

The beauty of vintage decor lies in its ability to bring uniqueness and character to a space. It's a creative rebellion against the monotony of mass-produced furniture, a nod to the past that adds depth to the present. And let's face it, it's a surefire way to impress your friends with your impeccable taste and eye for rare finds.

Character and Charm: Every vintage piece comes with its own story. A mid-century armchair or an Art Deco lamp isn't just a functional item; it's a piece of history that adds character to your space.

Sustainability: Embracing vintage is a stylish way to be eco-friendly. By choosing vintage, you're reducing waste and giving a new lease of life to beautiful pieces.

Quality Craftsmanship: They don't make them like they used to. Vintage furniture often boasts superior craftsmanship and quality materials, lasting longer than many contemporary pieces.

Here's how to get started:

- Mix, Don't Match: Blend vintage pieces with contemporary decor for a balanced look. It's all about creating a harmonious contrast.

- Start Small: If you're new to vintage, start with small items like lamps, mirrors, or decorative pieces before graduating to larger furniture.

- Condition Matters: Look for pieces in good condition. A little wear adds charm, but too much damage can be costly to repair.

Coco Chanel once said, "To be irreplaceable, one must always be different." This perfectly sums up the appeal of vintage decor. It's about creating a space that's as unique as you are.

But let's debunk a common myth: vintage doesn't mean stuffy or old-fashioned. It's about finding those timeless, classic pieces that bring a sense of elegance and history to modern living. It's the interior design equivalent of wearing a vintage Rolex with a modern suit - effortlessly cool and timelessly stylish.

Don't be afraid to repurpose. That vintage trunk can become a quirky coffee table, and those old wooden crates? They make great bookshelves. Vintage decorating is about thinking outside the (antique) box.

Remember, when it comes to vintage, it's not about creating a museum in your living room. It's about adding touches of the past that complement and enhance your current style. It's about making your space feel like a home, not a showroom.

Integrating vintage furniture and decor into your home is more than just a decorating trend; it's a way to express your personal style, to bring a sense of history and quality into your everyday life, and to make sustainable choices in your interior design. Each vintage piece in your home tells a story, your story, intertwined with the narratives of the past, creating a rich, dynamic atmosphere that is both personal and inviting. So, next time you come across a vintage piece, think of the stories it could tell and the charm it could add to your space. Remember, in the world of design, old can be the new 'new'.

The Vintage Furniture: An Adventure Through Time and Craftsmanship

Stepping into a place where each piece of furniture tells a story, where craftsmanship meets history. This is an era of vintage furniture—a realm where beauty and history intertwine, offering a unique aesthetic to any space. In this guide, we'll explore how to appreciate the artistry of vintage furniture, recognize various design eras, and value the uniqueness of each piece.

Appreciating Craftsmanship in Vintage Furniture
- Look Beyond the Surface: Learn to see the signs of quality craftsmanship, such as dovetail joints, solid wood construction, and hand-carved details.

- Understand the Maker's Mark: Discover the history behind

makers' marks and how they can reveal the origin and authenticity of a piece.

- Preservation and Care: Gain insights into maintaining vintage furniture to preserve its beauty and longevity.

Recognizing Design Eras and Styles

- Timeline of Styles: From Victorian to Mid-Century Modern, familiarize yourself with the key characteristics of each era.

- Spotting Authentic Pieces: Learn how to distinguish genuine vintage pieces from replicas or modern interpretations.

- Mixing Eras Tastefully: Get tips on integrating different styles and eras into your decor harmoniously.

Valuing the Uniqueness of Vintage Decor

- Storytelling Through Decor: Each vintage piece has a story. Discover how to use these stories to enhance the character of your space.

- Sustainable and Eco-Friendly Choices: Understand why choosing vintage is not only aesthetically pleasing but also environmentally responsible.

- Creating a Personalized Space: Learn how to select pieces that resonate with your personal style and create a unique ambiance.

Each section includes practical advice on selecting, maintaining, and integrating vintage furniture into modern living spaces, along with potential issues you might encounter and solutions to overcome them.

Have you ever wondered about the history behind that old armchair in your grandmother's house? Or how to make that vintage table fit in with your contemporary decor?

In conclusion, vintage furniture is not just about decorating spaces; it's about preserving history and craftsmanship. By understanding the artistry behind each piece, recognizing the significance of different design eras, and valuing the uniqueness of vintage decor, you can create a living space that is both aesthetically pleasing and rich in history. This adventure through the world of vintage furniture is not just about furnishings; it's about embracing a piece of history and making it a part of your story.

Rediscovering Charm: The Art of Acquiring and Revitalizing Vintage Furniture

Acquiring and refurbishing vintage furniture is not just about filling your space with objects; it's about reviving stories and crafting a unique aesthetic. This guide is your roadmap to discovering hidden gems and breathing new life into them, blending originality with functionality.

Sourcing Vintage Treasures

- Research and Planning: Begin with research. Familiarize yourself with different furniture styles, periods, and materials. This knowledge helps in identifying quality pieces.

- Where to Look: Explore thrift stores, estate sales, online marketplaces, and auctions. Each has its treasures waiting to be discovered.

- Inspecting for Quality: Check for sturdy construction, quality materials, and repair potential. Don't shy away from minor damages that can be fixed.

Refurbishing Techniques

- Cleaning and Preparing: Start with a gentle cleaning. Use mild soaps and avoid harsh chemicals that can damage old finishes.

- Restoration vs. Renovation: Decide whether to restore the piece to its original state or give it a modern twist. Respect the piece's history.

- DIY Techniques: Learn basic techniques like sanding, painting, and reupholstering. Use these skills to personalize your finds.

Balancing Originality and Functionality

- Respecting the Original Design: While adding personal touches, ensure that the changes don't overshadow the piece's inherent character.

- Adapting for Modern Use: Consider modifications that enhance functionality, like adding shelves or reinforcing frames, while maintaining the aesthetic.

- Mix and Match: Combine vintage and modern elements in your décor. This creates a dynamic and interesting space.

Avoiding Common Pitfalls

- Over-Restoration: Avoid overdoing the restoration process which can strip the piece of its vintage charm.

- Budget Management: Keep track of expenses. Restoration can become costly if not monitored.

- Space Planning: Ensure the piece fits in your space, both in size and style, before purchasing.

Celebrating Your Unique Space

- Displaying Your Finds: Arrange your refurbished pieces in a way that highlights their uniqueness and complements your living space.

- Sharing the Story: Every piece has a history. Share these stories with friends and family, adding a personal touch to your home.

The path in acquiring and refurbishing vintage furniture is a rewarding experience. It's about more than just furniture; it's about preserving history, expressing creativity, and crafting a living space that is uniquely yours. Remember, each piece tells a story, and now, it's a part of yours.

Vintage Charm in Modern Spaces: A Guide to Blending Old and New

Ever walked into a room that felt like a time capsule, yet seamlessly modern? That's the magic of integrating vintage items into contemporary spaces. This isn't just about decorating; it's about creating a story, a dialogue between the old and the new. Let's embark on this creative adventure together, transforming your space into a thematic, vintage-inspired haven.

Understanding Vintage: What is Vintage? Vintage pieces are those that capture the essence of a bygone era, typically at least 20 years old.

Choosing Your Era: Whether it's the roaring twenties or the funky seventies, pick a time period that resonates with your style.

Sourcing Vintage Treasures

- Where to Look: Explore thrift stores, antique shops, and online marketplaces.

- Quality over Quantity: Seek items in good condition and with authentic character.

Creating a Cohesive Look

- Mix, Don't Match: Combine vintage pieces with modern decor for a balanced look.

- Color Schemes: Stick to a consistent color palette to unify the space.

Consulting with Interior Designers

- Professional Insight: A designer can provide expert advice on optimal placement and integration.

- Cost-Effective Consultation: Many designers offer online consultations for budget-friendly advice.

Placement and Arrangement

- The Focal Point: Let a significant vintage piece anchor your room.

- Spatial Harmony: Ensure your layout is functional and aesthetically pleasing.

Creating Thematic Interiors

- Tell a Story: Each piece should contribute to the overall theme of the room.

- Accessorize Wisely: Use smaller vintage items to complement larger modern pieces.

Practical Advice and Potential Problems

- Maintenance: Vintage items may require special care. Research proper maintenance to preserve their charm.

- Balance: Avoid overcrowding. Too many vintage pieces can overwhelm a space.

Have you ever found a vintage piece that just spoke to you? Integrating such a find into your daily living space!

Incorporating vintage pieces into your contemporary space is more than just a design choice; it's a personal statement. It's about creating a home that tells a story, your story, through carefully selected pieces from different times. Remember, the goal is harmony, not just in design but in the stories these objects bring to your life. In blending the old with the new, you're not just decorating; you're curating a unique, timeless space that reflects your personal style.

Chapter 10
Vintage Vehicles and Automobiles

Driving a vintage vehicle isn't just about transportation; it's about experiencing a piece of history on wheels. It's the thrill of turning heads as you rumble down the street in a classic Ford Mustang or the feeling of stepping back in time when you slide into the leather seats of a 1960s Jaguar. For enthusiasts, these cars are more than just a means to get from A to B; they're rolling artworks, encapsulating the essence of eras gone by.

The allure of vintage vehicles lies not only in their aesthetic appeal but in the stories they carry. Each dent, scratch, and the well-worn seat tells a tale of adventures past. Owning a vintage car is like having a time machine in your garage, ready to transport you to a different era every time you hit the road.

- **Unmatched Style:** Vintage cars have a unique style that modern vehicles can't replicate. They are a testament to the craftsmanship and design of their time.

- **The Community:** The vintage vehicle community is a

tight-knit group, full of passionate individuals who share tips, stories, and parts.

- **Investment Potential:** Many vintage cars appreciate in value, making them not just a hobby but a potentially wise investment.

Here's how to get started in the vintage vehicle venture:

1. Do Your Research: Understand the maintenance needs and common issues of the model you're interested in.

2. Join Clubs and Forums: Connect with other enthusiasts for support, advice, and camaraderie.

3. Be Prepared for Maintenance: Owning a vintage car is a labor of love. These beauties require more care and attention than their modern counterparts.

As the legendary car designer Enzo Ferrari said, "The fact is I don't drive just to get from A to B. I enjoy feeling the car's reactions, becoming part of it." This perfectly encapsulates the experience of driving a vintage vehicle. It's not just transportation; it's an experience, a feeling, an adventure.

But let's be real: owning a vintage car isn't all glamorous road trips and admiring glances. It's also about grease-stained hands and weekend mornings spent under the hood. It's a commitment, almost like having a pet. You need to care for it, nurture it, and yes, sometimes talk to it nicely to coax it into starting on a cold morning.

Owning a vintage car also means becoming a part-time detective. Hunting down parts can be a challenge, but it's also part of the fun. It's about scouring internet forums, rummaging through swap meets, and sometimes, getting creative with solutions.

Remember, driving a vintage car is about enjoying the experience, not just reaching the destination. It's about the wind in your hair, the purr of the engine, and the feeling of connection to the road that modern cars just can't replicate.

Take note, vintage vehicles are like joining a secret club. It's a place of beauty, history, and passion. These cars aren't just modes of transport; they're pieces of history, each with its own story to tell. They represent a bygone era of design, style, and craftsmanship, offering an escape from the monotony of modern life. So, for those looking to add a little excitement and nostalgia to their lives, vintage vehicles might just be the answer. Remember, in the world of vintage cars, it's not about the speed; it's about the experience, the style, and the stories you create along the way.

Navigating the Timeless Charm of Vintage Vehicles: Automotive History and Passion

Welcome to the intriguing field of vintage vehicles. This realm is not just about cars; it's an adventure through history and passion, a blend of engineering artistry and cultural significance. Whether you're a seasoned collector or a curious enthusiast, understanding the vintage vehicle landscape is a fascinating adventure.

Historical Significance of Vintage Cars: Learn about the evolution of car design and technology from the early 20th century onwards. Vintage cars are more than just old vehicles; they're a window into the technological advancements and societal changes of their times. Explore significant models that defined automotive history, like the Ford Model T or the Volkswagen Beetle, and understand why they are revered.

The Market for Vintage Vehicles

- Valuation Factors: Discover what makes a vintage car valuable. Is it rarity, condition, historical significance, or a combination of these factors?

- Buying Tips: Gain insights into where and how to purchase vintage cars. Learn about auctions, private sellers, and online platforms.

The Allure of Automobile Memorabilia

- Collecting Beyond Cars: Understand the world of automobile memorabilia – from vintage ads and hood ornaments to classic car toys and garage signs.

- Emotional Connection: Explore why these items are not just collectibles but also hold sentimental value, evoking nostalgia and a sense of heritage.

Investing in Vintage Cars

- Financial Considerations: Learn about the investment potential of vintage cars. What makes a car a good investment, and what risks are involved?

- Maintenance and Care: Get practical advice on maintaining a vintage vehicle. Learn about restoration, preservation, and the importance of proper storage.

The Community and Culture

- Joining the Club: Discover the vibrant community of vintage car enthusiasts. Learn about clubs, meetups, and events where you can share your passion and gain knowledge.

- Preserving History: Understand your role in preserving automotive history. Each vintage car is a piece of history, and its maintenance is a contribution to cultural preservation.

Potential Issues and Solutions

- Market Fluctuations: The vintage car market can be volatile. Learn how to navigate these changes and make informed decisions.

- Restoration Challenges: Restoring a vintage car can be daunting. We'll provide tips on finding the right experts and sourcing authentic parts.

As we step into vintage vehicles, consider this: What draws you to these timeless machines? Is it the craftsmanship, the history, or the pure joy of driving something unique? This exploration is not just about cars; it's about connecting with a rich tapestry of history and emotion.

In conclusion, the realm of vintage vehicles is a captivating blend of history, art, and technology. Whether you're investing in a classic car, collecting memorabilia, or simply appreciating their beauty, you're part of a rich tradition that celebrates the milestones of automotive history. Embrace this adventure with curiosity and passion, and you'll find that vintage vehicles offer much more than just a ride – they're a gateway to a bygone era.

Vintage Vehicle Revival: The Art of Restoration and Regular Maintenance

Restoring a vintage vehicle is like unlocking a time capsule on wheels. It's not just about bringing a piece of history back to life; it's about cherishing a story that each car carries within its rusted parts and faded paint. For those with a passion for classic cars, understanding the essentials of restoration and maintenance is a rewarding venture. Let's dive into the world of vintage vehicles, where every nut and bolt has a tale to tell.

Restoration Essentials

- Starting Point: Identify the make and model of your vintage car. Research its history, original specifications, and common issues. This knowledge is your roadmap to successful restoration.

- Condition Assessment: Examine the vehicle thoroughly. Look for rust, damage, and missing parts. Your findings will guide the restoration process.

Develop a restoration plan. Prioritize tasks like structural repairs, engine refurbishment, and cosmetic restoration.

Regular Maintenance and Care

- Routine Checks: Regularly check and change fluids, inspect brakes, and ensure electrical systems are functioning. These small steps prevent major issues.

Store your vintage car in a dry, temperature-controlled environment. Use car covers and regularly clean and wax the vehicle to protect the paint.

Finding Parts and Services

- Parts Sourcing: Locate authentic parts. Utilize online forums, classic car clubs, and specialized dealers. Sometimes, customization or modern alternatives might be necessary.

- Choosing the Right Service: Not all mechanics are familiar with vintage models. Find specialists who have experience and passion for classic cars.

Restoration Realities

- Time and Budget: Be realistic about the time and money involved. Restoration is often more demanding than anticipated.

You may face parts scarcity or technical difficulties. Stay patient and seek advice from vintage car communities.

While keeping it authentic, add personal touches. Choose a unique paint color or interior design that reflects your style. Balance your personalization with respect for the car's original era and design.

Restoring and maintaining a vintage vehicle is a labor of love. It's about more than just the mechanical aspects; it's about connecting with history and creating a legacy. As you tighten each bolt and polish each chrome piece, you're not just restoring a car; you're reviving a piece of history. Remember, the process of restoration is as rewarding as the destination. So, are you ready to take the wheel and embark on this timeless adventure?

The Vintage Vehicle Management: Knowing the Legal, Insurance, and Social Landscapes of Classic Car Ownership

Welcome to the thrilling place of vintage vehicles! Embarking on this chapter promises not only an adventure into the past but also a unique challenge encompassing legal, insurance, and social aspects. Let's dive into the essentials of navigating this classic realm effectively.

Legal and Insurance Aspects: Each country has its own rules for vintage vehicles. Familiarize yourself with local regulations concerning emissions, safety features, and modifications. In some regions, vintage cars may be exempt from modern emissions standards.

Insurance Options and Valuations: Vintage cars require specialized insurance policies. Look for options that cover their unique value and usage patterns. Ensure your vehicle is accurately appraised to reflect its market value, historical significance, and condition. Regularly update your valuation to reflect any enhancements or market changes.

Managing Registration and Documentation: Maintain a detailed log of restoration, maintenance, and ownership history. This information is crucial for valuation and legal compliance. Some jurisdictions may offer special registration for vintage vehicles, often at a reduced cost but with usage limitations.

Using Social Media to Showcase Your Collection: Share your passion and connect with fellow enthusiasts through platforms like Instagram or Facebook. Capture your vehicle's best features and share its story, but be mindful of privacy and security concerns.

Stay informed about changing regulations to avoid legal pitfalls. Misjudging the value of your vehicle can lead to inadequate coverage. Consult with a specialist.

Ever wondered how to balance the allure of showcasing your vintage treasure on social media with privacy concerns? You're not alone!

As we reach the end of this chapter, remember that owning a vintage vehicle is not just about cherishing a piece of history, but also about understanding the nuances of its management. From legal compliance to social media savvy, mastering these aspects ensures your classic car adventure is as smooth and enjoyable as the ride itself.

Chapter 11
Vintage Collectibles and Toys

Collectible toys investment is like opening a treasure chest of nostalgia and history. It's not just about hoarding old stuff; it's about preserving memories, cherishing craftsmanship, and, let's not forget, the possibility of striking gold with a rare find. For the savvy collector, these relics from the past are not just playful reminders of yesteryears but potential investments that could pay off handsomely.

Vintage collectibles and toys are more than mere trinkets gathering dust on a shelf. They're time capsules, each with a story to tell. Whether it's a mint-condition Star Wars action figure from the '70s or a first-edition Barbie doll, these items represent a piece of history, a snapshot of culture, and, for many, a childhood unboxed.

The Joy of the Hunt: Finding vintage collectibles can be thrilling. It's the adult version of a treasure hunt, where flea markets, estate sales, and online auctions become your hunting grounds.

Nostalgia Factor: Collecting vintage toys and memorabilia often comes from a place of nostalgia, reconnecting us with our childhoods or eras we admire.

Investment Potential: While not all collectibles will appreciate in value, certain items can become highly sought-after, making them a smart investment.

Here's how to start your vintage collectible adventure:

1. Educate Yourself: Knowledge is power in the world of collectibles. Learn about the eras, the makers, and what makes certain items more valuable than others.

2. Condition is Key: The value of vintage items heavily depends on their condition. Look for items that are well-preserved, preferably with original packaging.

3. Network with Other Collectors: Join communities, both online and offline, to learn, trade, and stay informed about the market.

As American cultural anthropologist Margaret Mead insightfully said, "We are continually faced with a series of great opportunities brilliantly disguised as insoluble problems." This is particularly true in vintage collecting, where challenges like identifying authenticity or restoring items can turn into profitable opportunities.

But let's inject a dose of reality here: not every old toy in your attic is a hidden treasure waiting to be discovered. Sometimes, a cigar box full of old Hot Wheels is just that. The trick is to discern between what's merely old and what's genuinely collectible.

Vintage collecting also isn't about turning your home into an episode of 'Hoarders.' It's about curating a collection that has personal meaning and potential value. It's the difference between having a museum and a mausoleum in your living room.

Remember, collecting vintage items is partly an emotional investment. Each piece you collect should resonate with you on some level, whether it's a childhood memory, a fascination with a particular era, or an appreciation for fine craftsmanship.

Whether you're in it for the nostalgia, the thrill of the hunt, or the potential financial reward, collecting vintage toys and memorabilia is an adventure into the past, filled with stories, memories, and sometimes, unexpected windfalls. It's about connecting with history, reliving childhood joys, and appreciating the artistry and storytelling encapsulated in these timeless treasures. So, the next time you come across a vintage toy or collectible, think about the stories it could tell, the smiles it once brought, and the potential it holds. In the world of vintage collecting, every item has a past, and every past is a new adventure.

The Joy of Collecting: A Thrilling Adventure on Vintage Toys and Collectibles

Collecting a vintage toy and collectible holds a piece of history and a reservoir of nostalgia. This experience isn't just about acquiring objects; it's about embracing the stories and cultural significance behind them, creating a collection that's as diverse as it is meaningful. Whether you're a seasoned collector or just starting out, this guide will illuminate the joys, challenges, and rewards of this unique hobby.

Embracing the Nostalgia of Vintage Toys

Understanding the Appeal: Vintage toys are more than just relics; they're time capsules that transport us back to our childhoods. Remember the joy and wonder of your first toy? That's the essence of vintage toy collecting.

Identifying Key Pieces: Start by identifying toys that resonate with your personal history or cultural moments you cherish. Whether it's action figures from the 80s or classic board games, each piece has a story.

Learn the art of preserving these treasures. From proper storage to cleaning methods, ensure your collection stands the test of time.

The Cultural Significance of Collectibles

Impact on Popular Culture: Dive into how collectibles have shaped and been shaped by popular culture. From comic books to trading cards, these items reflect the evolving trends and values of society.

Collectibles as Investment: Understand the potential financial value of collectibles. While the primary joy comes from the nostalgia and personal connection, some items can become valuable over time.

Ethical Collecting Practices: Discuss the importance of ethical collecting. This includes avoiding counterfeit items and respecting the history and origins of the collectibles.

Building a Diverse and Meaningful Collection

Creating a Theme: Guide readers on how to choose a focus for their collection. This could be a specific era, type of toy, or even items related to a particular cultural phenomenon.

Networking with Fellow Collectors: Offer advice on joining collector communities. Share the joy of collecting with others, learn from their experiences, and find rare items.

Displaying Your Collection: Provide creative ideas for displaying collectibles. This can range from traditional shelving to more innovative methods that integrate them into home decor.

Collecting can be costly, so it's crucial to manage finances effectively. Also it is vital to discuss how to handle the challenge of finding rare items. So offering strategies such as networking, attending trade shows, and exploring online auctions can have a positive impact.

Each vintage toy and collectibles tells a story, reflecting not just personal memories but also broader cultural narratives. Whether you're drawn to the nostalgia, the community, or the potential investment, collecting can be a deeply rewarding hobby. Remember, the value of a collection isn't just in the items themselves, but in the joy and memories they bring. As you embark on or continue your collecting adventure, embrace the excitement, connect with others, and most importantly, have fun. This isn't just about accumulating objects; it's about cherishing pieces of history and personal significance.

The Art of Collectibles: A Path to Discovery and Verification

A hidden gem sitting unassumingly in a flea market, waiting for the keen eye of a collector. The world of collectibles is a treasure trove, where rare items hold stories and value beyond their physical appearance. This guide dives into the intricate process of evaluating and authenticating collectibles, a skill that can turn a hobby into a rewarding venture.

Identifying Rare and Valuable Items

- Observation Skills: Learn to spot what makes an item rare - be it age, condition, or uniqueness.

- Research Techniques: Utilize online databases and reference books to compare and contrast similar items.

- Networking: Engage with fellow collectors and experts to gain insights and share knowledge.

Authenticating Toys and Collectibles

- Understanding Marks and Signatures: Learn to recognize

manufacturer marks, artist signatures, and other indicators of authenticity.

- Condition Assessment: Assess the condition of an item, understanding how wear and restoration impact value.

- Professional Appraisals: When in doubt, seek expertise from certified appraisers.

Staying Informed About Market Trends

- Regular Research: Keep up with auction results, collector forums, and trade publications.

- Attending Shows and Conventions: Gain firsthand experience and knowledge from these gatherings.

- Online Communities: Participate in online forums and social media groups for up-to-date information.

Beware of reproductions and fakes. Always verify authenticity before making a purchase. Know that market values can fluctuate. Keep informed to understand current trends. Plus, preservation is key. Proper storage and care maintain the value of your collectibles.

Have you ever wondered about the story behind a vintage toy or the value of a rare collectible? Understanding these aspects can turn collecting into more than just a hobby.

As we've explored the nuances of evaluating and authenticating collectibles, it's clear that this path is as much about passion as it is about knowledge. Embrace the adventure of discovering hidden treasures and the satisfaction of understanding their true worth. Remember, each collectible isn't just an item; it's a piece of history, a fragment of art, and a part of your unique collection.

The Collector's Guide to Eternity: Preserving and Displaying Your Treasures

Step into the realm of preserving collectibles, a universe where your cherished possessions transcend time. This chapter is your compass in navigating the art of preservation and display, transforming your collection into a lasting legacy. Let's dive into the secrets that keep your collectibles timeless and your displays captivating.

Understanding Preservation Basics: Why Preserve? Your collectibles are more than items; they're stories, memories, and investments. Proper preservation ensures they withstand time, retaining their value and charm. On the other hand, light, temperature, humidity, and handling are the primary foes of collectibles. Learn to control these elements to protect your treasures.

Creating a Safe Haven for Your Collectibles

- Storage Solutions: Discover storage options like acid-free boxes, UV-protected display cases, and climate-controlled rooms.

- Handling With Care: Master the art of handling collectibles. Wear gloves, limit exposure, and ensure clean, safe environments.

The Art of Attractive Displays

- Showcasing with Style: Balance aesthetics and safety. Use creative layouts, themed displays, and strategic lighting to highlight your collection's uniqueness.

- Rotation is Key: Regularly rotate displayed items to reduce wear and exposure, keeping the collection fresh and engaging.

Documenting for Posterity

- Cataloging Techniques: Create a detailed catalog of your items, including descriptions, conditions, history, and value. This serves as a reference and a storybook of your collection.

- Digital Archiving: Utilize digital tools for archiving. Photographs, digital records, and cloud storage can immortalize your collection beyond physical limits.

Remember, be vigilant against overexposure, improper cleaning methods, and neglecting environmental controls. Have a plan for emergencies like fire, theft, or water damage. Insurance, backups, and recovery plans are vital.

Engaging with Your Collection

- Personal Connection: Reflect on what each item means to you. This emotional investment adds depth to your preservation efforts.

- Sharing Your Passion: Consider public displays, online forums, or collector groups to share stories and learn from others.

As we wrap up, remember that the essence of your collection lies in its stories, not just its physical form. By mastering these preservation and display techniques, you transform your collectibles into enduring narratives, echoing through time. Your treasures are not just for today; they're a dialogue with the future, a testament to your passion and care.

Chapter 12
Conclusion

It's clear that the path through the world of vintage is not just about buying and selling old items. It's about embracing a lifestyle, a mindset that values the past's craftsmanship and stories. This book has been your companion, guiding you through the many facets of the vintage world, from hunting treasures in dusty markets to the intricate art of restoration, from savvy marketing to global sourcing, and every nuanced step in between.

Throughout this adventure, you've been invited to see beyond the surface of vintage items. Each piece isn't just an object; it's a narrative, a fragment of history that speaks volumes. Whether it was the emotional connection to historical pieces in vintage markets or the thrill of breathing new life into forgotten treasures, every chapter in this book was a testament to the timeless appeal of vintage.

The art of restoration, as you've discovered, is a delicate dance between preserving history and making it relevant for today. It's about honoring the past while ensuring that these treasures continue to be appreciated in the present. You've learned not just the technicalities of restoration but also the joy and satisfaction it brings to revive and thrive, transforming old into gold.

Valuing your vintage collection isn't just a skill; it's an insight into the very soul of your items. It's been about understanding their worth, both in monetary terms and the stories they tell. This book has shown you how to navigate the complex world of appraisal, helping you to not just know the worth of your collection but to also build a legacy that transcends time.

Marketing your collection has been about crafting a narrative that resonates with your audience. You've learned the power of branding, digital strategies, and the importance of community in the vintage world. Each chapter on marketing has been a step towards turning your passion into a compelling story that captivates and engages.

Sourcing vintage internationally has opened your eyes to the global scope of this venture. It's about adapting to diverse market dynamics, building networks, and understanding the cultural significance of items from around the world. This part of the adventure has expanded your horizons, showing you that the world of vintage is indeed without borders.

The specialized areas of vintage photography, memorabilia, fashion, furniture, vehicles, and collectibles have each added depth to your understanding. These chapters have not only equipped you with knowledge but have also inspired you to explore new avenues, find your niche, and perhaps even ignite a passion for a specific category of vintage.

As you move forward, remember that vintage is ever-evolving. Each item you encounter is a new story waiting to be discovered, a new opportunity for business, and a new adventure. The knowledge you've gained from "Vintage Ventures" is not just a set of instructions; it's a foundation for your continued exploration in this fascinating world.

So, as you set down this book, know that your adventure in the world of vintage is just beginning. Take these lessons, these stories, and use them to carve out your unique path in the vintage world. Whether you're a collector, a restorer, a seller, or simply someone who appreciates the beauty and history of vintage items, remember that you are now part of a community that values the past and cherishes its stories.

Thank you for joining this adventure. May your path be filled with fascinating finds, rewarding restorations, and countless stories that connect you to the rich tapestry of history. Here's to your success in the vibrant world of vintage!

Printed in Dunstable, United Kingdom

65442858R00057